DATE DUE

MAR 1 4 69	
MAY 16 1994	

1/8/48

D1066280

LIFE ABIDING
AND ABOUNDING

BIBLE STUDIES IN PRAYER AND
MEDITATION

TABOR COLLEGE
LIBRARY
HILLSBORO, KANSAS

242

T463c

12785

BY

W. H. GRIFFITH THOMAS, D. D.

CHICAGO

THE BIBLE INSTITUTE COLPORTAGE ASSOCIATION

826 NORTH LA SALLE STREET

The Works of the
Rev. W. H. Griffith Thomas, D. D.
(With names of the publishers)

The Book of Genesis. A devotional commentary. Three vols. Vol. I, Gen. 1-25; Vol. II, Gen. 25-36; Vol. III, Gen. 36-50. Cloth, each net . . . $1.00
(*Fleming H. Revell Co., New York and Chicago.*)

The Epistle to the Romans. A devotional commentary. Three vols. Vol. I, Rom. 1-5; Vol. II, Rom. 6-11; Vol. III, Rom. 12-16. Cloth, each net . . . $1.00
(*Fleming H. Revell Co., New York and Chicago.*)

The Apostle Peter. Outline studies in his life and epistles. Cloth, net . . . $1.25
(*Fleming H. Revell Co., New York and Chicago.*)

Methods of Bible Study. A series of suggestions. Cloth, net 50
(*Fleming H. Revell Co., New York and Chicago.*)

Christianity is Christ. A summary of the evidences of Christianity in regard to the person and work of our Lord. Cloth, net 40
(*Longmans, Green & Co., New York.*)

The Catholic Faith. A manual of instruction for members of the Anglican Church. Cloth, net 50
(*Longmans, Green & Co., New York.*)

The Holy Spirit of God. Studies in the Biblical, historical, theological and practical aspects. Cloth, net . $1.75
(*Longmans, Green & Co., New York.*)

The Work of the Ministry. A text book for theological students and the younger clergy. Cloth, net . $1.50
(*George H. Doran Co., New York.*)

The Power of Peace. A meditation. Cloth, net . .40
(*Robt. Scott, Ltd., London, Eng.*)

The Prayers of St. Paul. Devotional and exegetical. Cloth, net 60
(*Charles Scribner's Sons, New York.*)

Royal and Loyal. Chapters on the spiritual life. Cloth, net 40
(*S. W. Partridge & Co., London, Eng.*)

Life Abiding and Abounding. Bible studies in Prayer and Meditation. Cloth, net 50
(*The Bible Institute Colportage Association, Chicago.*)

The Acts of the Apostles. Outline studies in Primitive Christianity. Cloth, net 50
(*The Bible Institute Colportage Association, Chicago.*)

All the books named above may be obtained from

The Bible Institute Colportage Association
826 North La Salle Street, Chicago

CONTENTS

CONTENTS

INTRODUCTION

" ABIDE in Me, and I in you." This is the clear command of our Lord. It is the last and culminating point of His will as revealed in the four great words: Come unto Me; Learn of Me; Follow Me; Abide in Me. It also expresses the intense desire of every Christian heart. "Oh that thou wouldest bless me indeed, and enlarge my coast, and that Thine hand might be with me, and that Thou wouldest keep me from evil, that it may not grieve me!" (1 Chron. iv. 10). "O that my ways were made so direct that I might keep Thy statutes" (Psa. cxix. 5, Prayer Book Version). And since God never commands without giving grace to obey, and never prompts the heart to desire what cannot be granted, we may be sure that the command to abide can be obeyed and that the desire to abide will be satisfied.

But how? The present little book is an endeavour to answer this question by calling attention to the twofold secret of abiding in Christ; the Word of God, and Prayer. The Christian life is set forth in Holy Scripture as pre-eminently a life of fellowship with God, and fellowship has for its essential quality the privilege of reciprocal communion; God speaks to the believer and the

believer speaks to God. This reciprocal communion is obviously summed up in the Bible and
Prayer; for it is through the Bible that God speaks
to us and through Prayer that we speak to God.
Everything in the Christian life, individual and
corporate, is somehow or other associated with the
Bible and Prayer. All the "means of grace,"
private and public, are connected with the Word
of God and with Prayer to God. Do we worship
in secret? It must be by prayer and by hearing
"what God the Lord will speak." Do we draw
near to God in company with His people? It can
only be as warranted by His Word and expressed
in Prayer. Do we participate in the Sacraments
of the Gospel? They derive their spiritual meaning and blessing as symbols and pledges of God's
revelation of Himself; they are "visible signs to
which are annexed promises."

Thus the Word and Prayer are never absent
from our life, and never far apart from each
other. In the life of Old Testament believers
they were always connected (Psa. xix.; cxix.).
In the life of our Lord they are constantly
found together (John xvii.). In the life of the
Early Church they are ever united (Acts iv. 24,
25; vi. 4). In relation to the Holy Spirit they
are inseparably connected (Eph. vi. 17, 18).
There is not a single channel of belief, not a single

element of experience, not a single pathway of service, not a single privilege, not a single grace, not a single hope, not a single possibility which is not in some way associated with the Word and Prayer. When these two are allowed to occupy in our life the place they occupy in God's purpose and plan for us, we have learnt the essential conditions, the blessed secret, the unspeakable joy of abiding in Christ and abounding for Christ.

The first chapter of this book is an amplification of an address delivered at Keswick. The second is a much-enlarged form of a Bible reading given at Northfield, which was subsequently issued as a booklet and is not now available in that form.

CHAPTER I

"MORE THAN MY NECESSARY FOOD"

IN the course of a conversation during a Keswick Convention a friend said, "Now, suppose someone yields himself to God and receives a blessing at one of these meetings, how is it possible for him to avoid relapsing into his former spiritual condition? Will it not be necessary for him to be propped up in some way?" I did not quite like the phrase "propped up," because it implied help from outside, rather than from within, but I replied: "There will, of course, be the danger of relapse; but together with the blessing comes the call to abide and to fulfill the conditions of abiding." My friend said: "What are these?" I answered: "Speaking after the manner of the body, they are three—pure air, good food, and constant exercise—the atmosphere of prayer, the food of the Word, and the exercise of obedience. When the act of surrender is thus transmuted into an attitude, the attitude will become a habit, and from the habit will come character."

Is not this the spiritual position and the spiritual need of very many Christians? They are conscious of having entered into a true spiritual relation to Christ; His grace is a reality, His presence is a joy, His peace is a comfort. But they are sadly afraid that these experiences will not last, that they will lose their present happiness and descend to a lower stage of spiritual life. What they need, therefore, and what they desire above all things, is to know the secret of remaining where and as they are; or, rather, the secret of both of *not* going back and also of going forward, the secret of abiding and abounding. They read in Scripture of "abiding in Christ" (John xv. 4), of "abiding in His love" (John xv. 10), of "continuing in prayer" (Col. iv. 2), of "always abounding in the work of the Lord" (1 Cor. xv. 58), of "going from strength to strength" (Psa. lxxxiv. 7). And very naturally and rightly they desire to know the secret of it all.

What, then, is the secret of abiding? The answer is, *faithfulness;* and when we connect together two passages of Holy Scripture, we may learn the secret of abiding in Christ.

"I have not hid thy righteousness within my heart" (Psa. xl. 10).

"Thy Word have I hid in mine heart" (Psa. cxix. 11).

1. THE LIFE FAITHFUL TO GOD

From the former of these two texts we must note very briefly the first secret of abiding, looked at from the outside. It is *faithfulness in the outward life.* "I have not hid thy righteousness within my heart." To use a New Testament phrase, this means the open confession of Christ as Lord. We know that from the moment of conversion, confession is our bounden duty—it is an absolute necessity to confess Christ as our Lord. Not only should we sanctify Him as Lord in our hearts, but confess Him as Lord by lip and life. This is the first requirement of every true life—the confession of God in Christ by word and by deed. Very often it will mean a confession, literally by the lip, of what Christ has been to us, of what God has done for our soul. But in particular, and always, it will be the confession of Christ in our life, that people may be able to see that Christianity does really make a difference, and that our life genuinely belongs to God. "I have not hid Thy righteousness within my heart."

And yet there will be the constant temptation to hide God's righteousness, and to avoid the confession of Christ by word and deed. This will, no doubt, be due in some cases to fear of man; we shall not have the courage of our convictions. We find it easy to confess Christ when we are among Christians; we may have found it delightful to trust Him in gatherings of His people, to send up our testimony and bear witness for Him. But it is possible, not to say probable, that we find it difficult to make the same confession when we are in our homes, and in our ordinary surroundings. The fear of man always brings a snare; it brings a snare to young converts, and indeed all through the Christian life to those who are tempted to avoid a confession of Christ. This is the devil's own snare—the trouble and difficulty of the spiritual duty of confession. And yet if it is not dealt with at once there can be nothing but spiritual defeat in our lives.

There is another reason, allied to this, that sometimes prevents us from confessing Christ, and tends to keep His righteousness within our heart. It is the fear lest in our home we should be convicted of inconsistency between what we say and what we are. How often Christian people ask clergymen, evangelists and other Christian workers to speak to their boys or girls, and when they are asked whether they have spoken themselves, the answer is, "No." It is probably because they are afraid that the boy or girl has seen something in the life of father or mother or friend which has not been true to Christ, and this inconsistency has been a hindrance. So there is the temptation, through our own inconsistency, to hide God's righteousness in our hearts.

The secret of abiding is obedience. If we would abide, we must obey; obey to the full measure of our light whatever God Himself says, and in this faithfulness will be the guarantee of a life that will go from strength to strength, from glory to glory.

2. THE WORD HIDDEN IN THE HEART

But the prime secret of abiding is *faithfulness in the inner life*. The second text, "Thy Word have I hid in mine heart," is the cause, of which the former is the effect. It is probable that some reader has been thinking as he reads of the call to faithful obedience; "Yes, but obedience, faithfulness, loyalty to the light—these things are difficult, almost insuperably difficult!" Difficult, they often are; mainly because we do not set about them in the right way. But they are not really difficult, certainly not insuperable if we understand the meaning of faithfulness in the inner life, which comes from our being devoted to the Word of God. "Thy Word have I hid in mine heart." Let us endeavour to find out first what will be the effect of hiding God's Word in our heart. Then we will seek to learn definitely what it means to hide God's Word in our heart, and how to do it.

The first result of hiding God's Word in our heart is *spiritual peace*. "Great peace have they which love Thy law, and nothing shall cause them to stumble" (Psa. cxix. 165, Hebrew). It is one of the most familiar facts of Christian experience that our inner peace is in exact proportion to our meditation on God's Word, the hiding of God's Word in our heart, and it is natural that this should be so, for the obvious reason that it is through the Word that we know God. In proportion as we come to know Him, we come to understand His will, and, with this, more and more of the fulness of His revelation in Christ Jesus. The outcome of this is peace. If, as we look back upon the last year, we are conscious that there has been an absence, to any extent, of this peace in our life, we may almost certainly put it down to the fact that we have not been too familiar with God through His Word, that we have not been often enough face to face with Him through His Word. "They that know their God shall be strong," and we can only know God through His Word. "Faith cometh by hearing, and hearing by the Word of God." And peace, too, cometh by hearing, and hearing by the Word of God.

"So to the heart that knows Thy love, O Purest!
  There is a temple, sacred evermore,
And all the babel of life's angry voices
  Dies in hushed stillness at its peaceful door.

Far, far away the roar of passion dieth,
  And loving thoughts rise calm and peacefully;
And no rude storm, how fierce soe'er it flieth,
  Disturbs the soul that dwells, O Lord, in Thee!"

Hiding God's Word in the heart is also the secret of *prayer*. There is a necessary and intimate connection between the Word of God and prayer. In the Bible God is speaking to us, while prayer is our speaking to God. In the Apostolic Church they said: "We will give ourselves to the ministry of the Word and to prayer." In two consecutive verses in Ephesians vi. the Spirit of God is associated with the Word and with prayer. The Word of God is called "the sword of the Spirit," and then we are told to "pray with all prayer and supplication in the Spirit"—the Spirit of God through the *Word;* the Spirit of God through *prayer.* George Müller once asked the question whether a Christian, in his daily morning devotions, should commence with prayer, or with the Bible; and he suggested that after a brief prayer for light and guidance, he should commence with the Bible, and not with prayer. This is a useful bit of advice from a master in the spiritual life, for the simple reason that God's Word is the fuel of our prayer. As we open the page in the morning, the promises prompt us to prayer, the examples incite us to prayer, the warnings urge us to prayer, the hopes of glory stir us to prayer— everything in the portion taken for our meditation can be turned into prayer. Let us try it, if we have never done so; let us start with the Word, and then turn to prayer. And I suggest that at night we reverse the process, start with prayer, and finish the day as we began, with the Word of God. Depend upon it, hiding God's Word in the heart is the secret of prayer, and the reason why our prayer-life is so weak and barren is that we do not know God through His Word. We do not lay hold of Him through this means. The Word is unfamiliar, and God is therefore afar off, and for this one reason our prayer is weak and unavailing. But the man who knows God through His Word becomes mighty in prayer every day.

Hiding God's Word in our heart is always the secret of *purity*. "Now ye are clean through the Word." In proportion as we come face to face with this Word will our inner and outer life be pure. There is nothing to compare with Scripture to purify motives. We may seem to have very beautiful motives when we are going about during the day; but when we get on our knees with the

Bible we are searched, and everything doubtful has to go. "If I regard iniquity in my heart, the Lord will not hear me." There is nothing like the Word of God for purifying the thoughts, the motives, the desires. The whole of the inner life of the believer becomes, and is kept pure, just in proportion as God's Word is hidden in our hearts.

There is an incident which illustrates this truth in one of those inimitable sermons to children by Dr. Richard Newton. It is the story of an old woman who had in her hand what seemed like a square sieve, with something in it, and she was holding the sieve in a stream, and allowing the water to pass through it. As she did this, a clergyman came along, and stopped to see what the old woman was doing. She turned round and looked at him, and the moment she saw him she said: "Oh, sir, I am very glad to see you." He replied: "I do not know how you can be; I am a stranger in these parts, and I was not aware that I was known." "Well," said she, "I heard you preach a sermon many years ago which was blessed to my soul, and I have been a different woman ever since." "I am thankful to hear it," replied he, "what was the text?" "I don't remember the text," she added. "But," said he, "it is very curious that a sermon should have been blessed to your soul, and yet that you cannot remember the text." "Well," she replied, "you see, I have got some wool in this sieve, and my mind is very much like the sieve, which is full of holes. The water runs through the sieve, but as it runs through it cleanses the wool. Now that text of God's Word went through my mind, and though it did not stop there long enough for me to remember it, yet as it went through it cleansed me, and I have been a different woman ever since."

We cannot remember the fifty-two or the one hundred and four sermons we hear every year, but each time we hear the Word, it can go into and through our soul and cleanse it. Though we may not remember this or that sermon, yet if the sermon is based on the Word of God, it will have done its work in cleansing and purifying heart and soul. And so also, in our private devotions, it is impossible to keep in memory everything that God tells us from day to day; but each message as it comes does its work, and every day we need further cleansing. Hiding God's Word in the heart is the secret of purity.

It is also the secret of *power*. The Word of God is the prime secret of power in the Christian life—power to resist temptation, power to overcome sin, power to do God's work whatever it may be, power proportioned to the work we have to do.

And that grace of God which comes through hiding His Word in our hearts is always sufficient for all things, that we may abound unto every good work. The reason of our powerlessness in Christian service, against temptation, in the midst of evil, and in the face of all the problems of to-day, is, that we are not enough alone with God through His Word.

Hiding God's Word in our heart is the secret of spiritual *perception*. The man who knows God through His Word sees and understands God's will as no one else does. It seems to be a mark of a growing, maturing Christian that he is *able to understand*. The last Epistle of St. Peter lays great stress on "knowledge"; the first Epistle of St. John has as its keynote the word *know*. There are three grades or stages of the Christian life in that Epistle: "I write unto you, little children, because your sins are forgiven. I write unto you, young men, because you are strong. I write unto you, fathers, because you know." But when the Apostle repeats these appeals he adds something different about the children, and about the young men, but nothing about the fathers. He just repeats exactly what he had said about them, because there is nothing else to say. "I write unto you, fathers, because ye have *known* Him that is from the beginning." If we read the Epistles of St. Paul to the Ephesians, the Philippians, and the

TABOR COLLEGE LIBRARY HILLSBORO KANS

Colossians, and note down the various references to *knowledge*, we shall find that *full* or *mature knowledge* is the keynote of those writings; as though St. Paul would suggest to us that knowledge, spiritual understanding, perception, is the mark of a ripening and growing Christian. This perception can only come from abiding closely with God in His Word, and hiding that Word in our heart. The man who gives himself to daily thought and prayerful meditation on God's Word possesses a degree of spiritual perception out of all proportion to his intellectual capacity or attainment, judged from the standpoint of things natural. Dr. James Hamilton says in one of his sermons that "a Christian on his knees sees farther than a philosopher on his tip-toes." The prayerful Christian, however illiterate he may be, according to the world's idea, can often teach the educated man profound lessons.

And this has a very definite application to certain modern tendencies. If people kept more closely than they do to the Word of God, they would not be in danger of going aside to any of the various theories and "isms" of the present day. Thus, if a man abides in God's Word in daily prayerful meditation, he will never be deceived by Christian Science, which, as we know, is neither Christian nor scientific. In the same way the man

12785

who keeps close to God's Word will never be
deceived by the speciousness of Spiritualism. So
it is also with other aspects of error which we
rightly regard as dangerous. In every case where
a man who was once a professing Christian, and a
Christian worker, has taken up Christian Science
—if we found out everything that could be found
out about him, we should discover that his change
of opinion was due to his neglect of this Book.
So for the power of spiritual perception let us
keep close to the Scriptures, and then we shall not
go wrong.

Hiding God's Word in our heart is the secret of
spiritual *progress*. "If ye continue in My Word,
then are ye My disciples indeed." The man who
grows in grace is the man who grows in knowledge,
and the man who grows in knowledge is the man
who keeps close to God through His Word. For
spiritual progress this is the secret: "Thy Word
have I hid in mine heart." Whenever a Christian
is growing in grace, experiencing more joy in
Christ, more rest of soul, more peace of heart,
more knowledge of truth, more blessing in service,
more hope in trial, more endurance in suffering,
the explanation is as clear as it is simple. He is
spending more time with his Bible. There is no
need for spiritual declension, no necessity for back-

sliding, no warrant for anything but ever-joyous progress as we go from strength to strength through the year. But this will only be through hiding God's Word in our heart.

Hiding of God's Word in our heart is the secret of spiritual *permanence*. Daniel was taken as a boy of fourteen years old to Babylon, and he lived there until he was ninety-one; apparently he never went home to Jerusalem, but was in Babylon all those years, and we are told that Daniel *continued*. This may well be applied to moral and spiritual continuance, for we know how true this was of him. In the same way we may say that there is a Daniel in the New Testament, St. Paul. "Having therefore obtained help of God, I *continue* unto this day." Our Lord said, *"Continue* ye in My love." "If ye *continue* in My Word." The secret of continuance and permanence in the Christian life is hiding God's Word in our heart.

Let us then take this Word for our daily meditation, and we shall soon see in it the secret of everything in the Christian life.

> "And the daily load grows lighter,
>   The daily cares grow sweet,
> For the Master is near, the Master is here,
>   I have only to sit at His feet."

3. THE METHODS OF MEDITATION

Now comes the question, How is this to be done? Let me in the very simplest and most old-fashioned way try to show how this may be.

Our hiding of God's Word must be a *daily* practice. At the time of my ordination in 1885, we were being addressed by Dr. Hessey, then Archdeacon of Middlesex, and he said to us: "Whatever is true of you and your ministry, you ought to know your Greek Testament, and if you will read, in the original, the second lesson selected for that purpose in the Church of England service, you will find that it will cover almost the whole of the New Testament in a year, and so every year of your ministry you will be able to read through your Greek Testament." Some of us took that simple and, as it seemed, very obvious hint, and no one can tell the joy and blessing it has been to use the lesson as a daily portion for morning meditation. If we do not meditate upon God's Word daily we shall suffer in our spiritual life. In proportion as we neglect it there will be weakness in our souls. Whether in the Greek Testament or not, there should be systematic daily meditation. Some of us may belong to the Bible Prayer Union, the members of which read right through the Bible in three and one-quarter years. Many follow that course, and find it a great delight. Others prefer the Scripture Union, while still others have their own methods. But whatever method it may be, it ought to be used systematically and daily.

Our use of God's Word should be *direct;* and by direct use I mean first-hand meditation. Thank God for all helps! But let us remember that the greatest of all helps is a first-hand study of, and meditation on, the Word itself, as we now have it, and not as other people have provided it for us in *Daily Light,* or in any other way. Whatever we do in regard to helps, they must be secondary, and not primary. It has often been curious to me to note how many people there are with names commencing with "M," who have given us delightful books of meditation—Moule, Macgregor, Morgan, Mantle, Murray, Moore, Meyer. Their books have been a blessing to very many. But I know another "M" which is far more important and therefore better than all these. It is found in the 104th Psalm—"*My* meditation of Him shall be sweet" (see verse 34). This is the meditation that must ever come first, *my own,* what I get direct from God. Let us look again at this text, made as clear as possible for our guidance. "MY meditation"—my own, not someone else's. Shall we then despise the others? God forbid! We shall appropriate and enjoy all they can teach us, but it will be because we have come face to face with God ourselves, first of all.

For our devotional reading and meditation we should use unmarked Bibles. I know it is customary to have marked Bibles, full of suggestions, so that the moment we open a page we are directed to certain passages and lines of thought. But in meditating upon these we are almost inevitably feeding upon the old manna, and unless our mind is particularly independent, we shall pretty certainly get the same food again and again. What we need is to be able to open to a passage like the 23rd Psalm, and get from it something absolutely fresh. For this purpose we must have an unmarked Bible, and then afterwards we can put into our marked Bible all the discoveries or "finds" we have made during meditation. So for devotional purposes let our Bible be unmarked.

In this connection, is it not true that the greatest danger in the life of a minister or other Christian worker is that of reading the Bible for other people? When we open our Bible and God shows us something, we say: "That will do for my sermon next Sunday, or for my Bible class." But for the time being, never mind sermon or Bible class; let us ask ourselves: "What does this portion say to *me?*"

Our reading of God's Word must be *definite*. "What does it say to *me?*" This is the difference between study and meditation. A good definition of meditation is "attention with intention." Study is attention, but meditation is attention and also intention. What are the stages or elements of true meditation? They are five in number:—

1. The careful reading of the particular passage or subject, thinking over its real and original meaning.

2. A resolute application of it to my own life's needs, to conscience, heart, mind, imagination, will; finding out what it has to say to *me*.

3. A hearty turning of it into prayer for mercy and grace, that its teaching may become part of my life.

4. A sincere transfusion of it into a resolution that my life shall reproduce it.

5. A whole-hearted surrender to, and trust in God for power to practise it forthwith, and constantly throughout the day.

Meditation is, thus, first of all, thought; then it means application to myself; then prayer for grace; then the yielding of the heart to God; and then rising up to obey Him. This is the real meaning and purpose of definite hiding of God's Word in our heart. This is what it meant to Daniel. When he had had the Divine vision (in chap. viii.)

he said: "Afterward I rose up, and did the king's business." After the vision of God in His Word, we have to rise up and do the King's business. This is what is meant by hiding God's Word in our heart; it must be daily, direct, and definite.

As a practical outcome let the following suggestions be offered for the devotional use of the Bible:—

1. Open all such occasions with prayer for the Holy Spirit's light (Psa. cxix. 18).

2. Ask to be guided to some definite thought for *yourself*.

3. Dwell prayerfully on this thought thus given —Is it a counsel? A precept? A warning? A promise? An experience? A command?

4. When its meaning is clear, use it as the basis of a prayer for grace to realise it in experience.

5. Yield the whole soul in full surrender to its truth and power.

6. Link it on to truths already known, and thereby strengthen the chain of experience.

7. Trust God to reproduce it in your life that day.

Nothing in this world can ever be substituted for daily, direct, definite hiding of God's Word in our heart. We cannot make up for failure in our

devotional life by redoubled energy in service for
Christ. Our work will never rise higher than our
devotional life. As water never rises above its
level, so what we do never rises above what we are.
And in our preaching we shall never take people
one hair's breadth beyond our own spiritual attainment. We may point to higher things, we may
"allure to brighter worlds," but when we "lead the
way" we shall only take them just as far as we
ourselves have gone. Our personal contact with
the Word of God will thus be an exact test of our
discipleship and our character. Christianity is
largely a matter of condition of soul; stress is laid
on character and character is power. But character requires solitude for growth; solitude is "the
mother-country of the strong." And yet solitude
without the Bible tends to develop morbidity, while
with the Bible it guarantees vitality and power.
So let us remember that all the activity in the
world, all the reading of other books, all our public worship can never take the place of this daily,
definite, direct hiding of God's Word in our heart.

Granted this, failure in the Christian life is
absolutely impossible. The Word in the heart is
the secret of everything. If a man will spend a
little time with God every day of his life, he will
go on from strength to strength; his knowledge,
his capacity, and power for good will ever increase

and deepen, and his life will be one of widening blessing to others and of glory to God.

In the course of a Bible reading some years ago, I ventured to make this assertion: I said that if there were five hundred people outside that church, and each one of them was a backslider, I would undertake to say, although they were all strangers to me, that every one had become a backslider through neglect of the Bible. After the meeting was over a lady said to me: "I cannot understand how it is that every one of the five hundred should have become a backslider through neglect of the Bible." "Well, now," said I, "let us see. Have you got a looking-glass in your bedroom?" She answered, "Yes." "Do you use it?" I asked. "Yes," she replied. "Suppose," I went on, "you did not use it for a week, would you be quite sure that your personal appearance would be such as you would like your friends to see?" "No," said she. "Now, in the Epistle of St. James," I remarked, "the Bible is spoken of as a mirror in which we see ourselves; and if we do not open that Book we cannot be sure of our spiritual appearance. 'In Thy light shall we see light.'" Then I said: "You have soap and water in your bedroom?" She began to smile, and said, "Yes." "Do you use it?" I asked. She smiled a little more, and I added: "Suppose you did not use it for a week, would you be quite sure of your personal appearance, especially if you lived in London?" "No," she said. "Now," I pointed out, "in the Epistle to the Ephesians the Word is called 'water'; 'The washing of water by the Word.' As water is to the body, so is the Word of God to the soul. It cleanses. If we do not practise cleansing we cannot be clean." Then I added, "When you go downstairs I take it that you have your breakfast?" She said, "Yes." "Now suppose," said I, "you did not eat your breakfast, and went without food for a few days, you know what the result would be. The reason why people are ill in body is because they are 'below par,' and they thereby become a prey to the microbes that come in their millions. If people are strong and vigorous, they may consume microbes by the thousand and suffer no harm. But if we are below our normal state of health, and the microbes enter and find something to attach themselves to in our body, the result is illness and disease. So it is in the spiritual life. God's Word is spoken of as food, milk and honey —food to eat, milk to drink, and honey for "dessert." There is an entire meal in God's Word. If we eat God's Word we are strong, but if we do not, we become a prey to the microbes of temptation; they find us below spiritual 'par,' and the result is, we fail and become ill and diseased. But when we can say, with Jeremiah, 'Thy words were found, and I did eat them, and Thy Word was unto me the joy and rejoicing of mine heart,' when we use the water and the food and the mirror found in God's Word, there can be no backsliding.'' She said, "I see it now!"

As long as we keep the mirror before us in which we see ourselves, at the same time "beholding as in a glass the glory of the Lord," we become transformed. As long as we use the water of God's Word for the cleansing of our inner life, and the milk and honey of God's Word as the food of our souls, it will be absolutely impossible for us to backslide, while it will be blessedly possible for us to go on from grace to grace, and from strength to strength; and it shall be true of us as of the Psalmist: "The law of his God is in his heart; none of his steps shall slide." The law of God in the heart makes us as "the righteous man" who "shall hold on his way; and he that hath clean hands shall be stronger and stronger."

All that has been said may be summed up in the words of Job: "I have esteemed the words of His mouth more than my necessary food"; and of Jeremiah: "Thy words were found, and I did eat them"; and of the Psalmist: "How sweet are Thy words to my taste!" The Bible must be our daily food if we are to be strong and vigorous. Not quantity, but quality, determines the nutritive value of food. What we must emphasize is capacity to receive, power to assimilate, and readiness to reproduce. As someone has well put it, the process is three-fold—infusion, suffusion, transfusion.

The Word thus becomes all-sufficient and all-powerful in our life—the mirror to reveal (James i.); the water to cleanse (Eph. v.); the milk to nourish (1 Peter ii.); the strong meat to invigorate (Heb. v.); the honey to delight (Psa. cxix.); the fire to warm (Jer. xxiii.); the hammer to break and fasten (Jer. xxiii.) the sword to fight (Eph. vi.); the seed to grow (Matt. xiii.); the lamp to guide (Psa. cxix.); the statute book to legislate (Psa. cxix.); and the gold to treasure in time and for eternity (Psa. xix).

Three or four paragraphs of the above have been taken from the author's *Methods of Bible Study*.

CHAPTER II

"THE CHRISTIAN'S VITAL BREATH"

THE Christian religion rests upon two great facts. The first is, that God has spoken to man in the Lord Jesus Christ, and still speaks by the Holy Spirit. The second is, that man can hear God's voice and speak to Him in return. Divine Revelation and Human Response to it are thus the two foundations of all true life. The voice of God to man is heard in the Word of God applied by the Holy Spirit. The voice of man to God is mainly expressed in prayer.

We have already considered the former of these two subjects, the Revelation of God in His Word in its relation to the Christian life. To the latter we now turn our attention in order to discover some of the secrets of that most wonderful of all human powers, the ability to speak to the "Lord who made heaven and earth."

Prayer has always been prominent in the lives of the people of God. Whether we study the lives of the men of God recorded in the Bible, and look at the history of Abraham, Isaac, Jacob, Moses, Joshua, Samuel, David, Hezekiah, Isaiah, Ezekiel, Daniel, Peter, Paul, and John; or whether we take up some of the great biographies of the Christian centuries, and read of Augustine, Luther, Rutherford, Brainerd, McCheyne, and a host of others, we can easily see the prominence of prayer in every instance, and this prominence is a sure sign of its necessity, importance, and blessedness. Above and beyond all other proofs is the example of our Lord, true "Son of Man," whose life on earth was a life of prayer. In the second Gospel, which, as is well known, is pre-eminently the record of His constant service and marvelous activity, there are no less than ten occasions recorded of His retirement for prayer and communion with God.

In view of the paramount importance of prayer let us consider some of the inexhaustible wealth of New Testament teaching connected with it, giving ourselves mainly to the study of the various words and phrases associated with prayer in the Word of God.

1. Aspects of Prayer

Prayer is a *sense of need* (δέησις and δέομαι and their cognates). The substantive δέησις occurs nineteen times and the verb δέομαι twenty-three times. The former is translated in Ephesians vi. 18 by "supplication," and the meaning there, as elsewhere, is the acknowledgment of a sense of need. This is, perhaps, the most elementary idea of prayer, and it may be well for us to ask ourselves whether we realise our need when we pray. Is it a fact that when we come before God in prayer we have a definite and real consciousness of need? Is there a *vacuum* in our spiritual life, so that we feel we must be filled with the presence and grace of God? It is well for us to test ourselves after a season of prayer, and to ask ourselves, What have I been asking for? Do I remember the petitions I have offered, and have they really been the expression of my sense of genuine need? Even the most mature believer may well go back from time to time to this simple and elementary touchstone of the reality of his prayers.

Prayer is an *expression of desire* (αἰτέω, αἴτημα). The Greek words are found altogether in some seventy-four passages. "Let your requests (αἰτήματα) be made known unto God" (Phil. iv. 6) is one of these, and *"Ask* (αἰτεῖτε), and it shall be given you" (Matt. vii. 7) is another.

"Prayer is the soul's sincere desire."

The thought here is associated with the attitude of a petitioner, one who has a deep desire, and expresses it in prayer. Does this accord with our experience of prayer?

"What things soever ye *desire*" (Mark xi. 24).
Do our prayers truly voice our strongly felt desire?
If so, we know a little of what prayer means,
but if there is no real desire our words count for
nothing.

Prayer is a *spirit of humility*. This aspect of
prayer comes before us in one passage only (Heb.
v. 7) where the word ἱκετηρία refers to our Lord's
prayer in Gethsemane, and is translated in our
Authorised Version "supplications." "Who in the
days of His flesh, when He had offered up prayers
and supplications with strong crying and tears
unto Him that was able to save Him from death,
and was heard in that He feared." The picturesque
and beautiful thought imbedded in the word is
suggested by the fact that it was originally used
for the olive branch which a suppliant had in his
hands as he came towards a king from whom he
desired some favour. He thus grounded his application on his attitude as a suppliant, on his
humility. From the application of the word to the
olive branch came its use to express the thing
signified by the olive branch, the spirit and attitude of a suppliant. How beautiful is the word
in connection with our Lord's earthly life of prayer
as an indication of His true and perfect manhood.
The word sums up the teaching of the Epistle to

the Hebrews as to the perfect oneness of our Lord
with us in His humanity (apart from sin). "He
was made like unto His brethren in all things"
(Heb. ii. 17 and iv. 15). In Him, and like Him,
we too come before God as suppliants. We approach the King of kings (Who is none the less
King of kings because He is our Father in Christ
Jesus) in the merits of our Lord, with the olive
branch of peace made through the blood of His
Cross. Is this the spirit of our prayers? It is
possible to abuse the covenant of grace and to become unduly familiar with God and holy things.
While it is true that we have entrance to the
presence of God in Christ, it is "entrance into the
holiest." "Holy and reverend is His Name."
There is far too little of the spirit of humility and
reverence in our prayers. We must take the shoes
from off our feet, for the place whereon we stand
is indeed holy ground.

"Prayer is an *attitude of consecration.* In no
less than one hundred and twenty-five passages
of the New Testament we find the words προσευχή
and προσεύχομαι used to express the idea of prayer.
It is by far the commonest word denoting prayer
to God, and its root idea is consecration. It is
compounded of εὐχή, "a vow" and πρός, "turning
towards"; and means the turning of ourselves to
God in surrender. It is an attitude of worship ex-

pressed in prayer. It will suffice to refer to Acts
i. 14 and x. 9 as two out of the many passages.
When we remember the large number of occur-
rences of these words we can readily see what is the
normal attitude of the believer in prayer. It is the
attitude of a worshipper, of one who is turned
towards God with all his heart and soul. This is
one of the essential secrets of prayer, the soul's
whole-hearted surrender and consecration. David
said, "If I regard iniquity in my heart, the Lord
will not hear me" (Psa. lxvi. 18); and if the soul
is unwilling to surrender all to God and to turn
to Him in whole-hearted devotion, our prayers will
never receive an answer. On the other hand, when
we turn to God in submission and dedication, the
initial act becoming a permanent attitude of the
life, our prayers prevail, and "we have the petitions
that we desired of Him," (1 John v. 15).

Prayer is a *privilege of fellowship*. This thought
is suggested by the rare word ἐντεύξις, which occurs
only twice in the New Testament (1 Tim. ii. 1.;
iv. 5), being rendered "intercession" in the former,
and "prayer" in the latter passage. The verb
associated with this substantive (ἐντυγχάνω) is found
in Romans viii. 27, 34; xi. 2; Hebrews vii. 25, and
is invariably rendered by "intercede" or "make
intercession." It is necessary to remember that
in the course of time, since our Authorised Version

IABOR COLLEGE LIBRARY
HILLSBORO KANSAS 67063

was given to us, the meaning of the word "intercession" has become modified. We are now accus-
tomed to limit the word to prayer for others, but
there was no such limit three hundred years ago.
In 1 Timothy iv. 5, the Greek word cannot mean
prayer for others only, and is probably to be
limited to prayer for one's self.

The original word* implies the meeting of two
friends who talk together and ask each other for
something, thus realising and expressing their fellowship. The word suggests the thought of prayer
as *familiar speech,* as to the privilege of close
friendship and intimate fellowship. This is one
of the deepest and most precious aspects of prayer.

"Truly our fellowship is with the Father, and
with His Son Jesus Christ" (1 John i. 3). It was
this fellowship and holy familiarity of friendship
that Enoch and Noah enjoyed as they "walked
with God." It was this which led to Abraham
being called "the friend of God," and it was
familiar intercourse with God which led to Moses
being described as one "whom the Lord knew face
to face" (Deut. xxxiv. 10). This is the culminating point of Christian privilege and opportunity,
fellowship with God and the power of intimate
and blessed intercourse in prayer.

Prayer is a *spirit of enquiry.* The word sug-
gesting this is ἐρωτάω (John xvi. 23). Our Lord

---

*Trench, *Synonyms of the New Testament*, p. 190.

said to His disciples, "In that day ye shall ask
Me *no questions*," i.e., in the day of the Holy
Spirit's full revelation the disciples would have no
need to make enquiries of their Master; all the
things which had troubled them would be made
clear. And yet this word is used once in the New
Testament in connection with prayer. In 1 John
v. 16 we read of "sin unto death," *i.e.*, not any particular sin, but *sin,* the state and condition of evil.
The Apostle then goes on to say, "I do not say
that he should *make enquiry* (ask a question) concerning this." The thought suggested is that of
the believer asking questions, seeking light on a
difficulty, "Lord, what is the meaning of this?"
This is part, and a most precious part, of our life
of privilege, that of going to the Lord in prayer,
seeking light and explanation. One of the most
beautiful illustrations of this is found in the story
of the Last Supper as recorded by St. John. When
John was leaning on the bosom of Jesus, Peter,
wishing to know who was about to betray their
Master, beckoned to John to ask Jesus who it was.
In the Revised Version we read, "Then John, leaning back, *as he was,* on Jesus' breast, said, Lord,
who is it?" He was already leaning on the bosom
of his Master, and he had no need to come closer:
so he simply leaned back and asked, "Lord, who
is it?" This is the true attitude of the believer,

in such close fellowship with Christ that he can simply ask his Master about any difficulty, and seek for the explanation. Prayer in this sense is not for gifts or grace so much as for guidance and light. The Lord "will be enquired of" for this. He delights to have us take our difficulties and problems to Him. He Himself said, *"Shall I hide from Abraham that thing which I do?"* and "Henceforth I call you not servants; for the servant knoweth not what his lord doeth: but I have called you friends; for all things that I have heard of My Father I have made known unto you." Let us treasure and use the privilege of fellowship more and more. "Were half the breath vainly spent" in telling our difficulties to others used in telling the Lord about them, we should soon have fewer problems and many more solutions.

Prayer is a *bond of union*. In Matthew xviii. 19 we read, "If two of you shall agree on earth as touching anything that they shall ask." The word translated "agree" is συμφωνέω, from which we get our word "symphony." "If two of you shall symphonize," the two voices blending in beautiful agreement. Prayer, therefore, is more than the request of one individual, and is kept from being solitary and even selfish by being exercised in union with others. Union in prayer is one of the most blessed and potent influences of true Christian life, and we cannot have too much united prayer.

The "symphony" of God's people in prayer is the sure harbinger of spiritual blessing from God.

These are seven of the most prominent aspects of prayer as revealed in the New Testament, and we may use them as a touchstone of our ideas of prayer, and also the reality of our own prayer-life. They will show us what God means by prayer, and what He has for us of spiritual blessing by means of it. As the Puritan Trapp quaintly says, "God respecteth not the arithmetic of our prayers, how many they be; nor the rhetoric of our prayers, how long they may be; nor the music of our prayers, how methodical they be; but the divinity of our prayers, how heart-sprung they are. Not gifts, but graces, prevail in prayer."

> "To stretch my hand and touch Him,
>   Though He be far away;
> To raise my eyes and see Him
>   Through darkness as through day;
> To lift my voice and call Him—
>   This is to pray!
>
> To feel a hand extended
>   By One Who standeth near;
> To view the love that shineth
>   In eyes serene and clear;
> To know that He is calling—
>   This is to hear!"

2. SUBJECTS OF PRAYER.

From the thought of what prayer is we naturally turn to consider the teaching of Holy Scripture as to the subjects of prayer, what we should pray for, the main and outstanding petitions warranted and encouraged in the New Testament. What are the things laid down in Scripture as to which there can be no doubt that we may and should pray to God?

Spiritual Adjustment. 2 Cor. xiii. 9, "This also we wish, even your perfection." The word means "adjustment," the proper and due adjustment of the soul's relation to God. This word and its cognates occur pretty frequently and the meaning is invariably the same. "That the man of God may be *adjusted*" (2 Tim. iii. 17). "For the *adjusting* of the saints" (Eph. iv. 12). The word is used of *"mending* their nets" in Matthew iv. 21, and the above passage in Ephesians iv. 12 might literally be rendered, "for the *repair* of the saints." The people of God often need spiritual "repair," their nets to be "mended," and this was the prayer of St. Paul for Corinth, where his anxieties about the spiritual life of the Church had been so great. "This I wish, even your *repair.* When anything has become wrong in the life of a believer the primary necessity is re-adjustment. As an arm

which has been dislocated must be set before
health and strength can return, so the soul must
be reinstated in a right position with God before
a healthful condition again becomes possible. The
cause of so much dryness, weakness, powerlessness, in many a Christian life is that the soul is
out of adjustment. This is one of our true aspirations in prayer, and no one can exaggerate its importance and necessity. For spiritual re-adjustment and repair, for re-instatement in the right
position, for vigour of life, let us be much in prayer.
Prayer brings us into the presence of God and enables us to see what is wrong. Prayer then brings
to us the healing, forgiving grace of God which
adjusts the soul and places it once more in that
living union and communion with our Lord, from
which all vigour, blessing, and joy naturally flow.

"Drop Thy still dews of quietness,
    Till all our strivings cease:
Take from our souls the strain and stress,
And let our ordered lives confess
    The beauty of Thy peace.

Breathe through the pulses of desire
    Thy coolness and Thy balm;
Let sense be dumb, its heats expire:
Speak through the earthquake, wind, and fire,
    O still small voice of calm!"

Spiritual Progress. Col. iv. 12. Epaphras prayed for those at Colosse, that they might "stand perfect and complete in all the will of God." The word "perfect" here, as elsewhere, means mature, full-grown, ripe in experience (τέλειος). There is no allusion whatever in the word or context to the entire absence of sin or sinlessness. St. Paul frequently uses the word to denote a fully developed or ripening Christian as distinct from a new beginner, a "man in Christ" from a "babe." In 1 Corinthians ii. 6, he writes, "We speak wisdom among them that are *"mature,"* those that have reached or are approximating towards the end or goal (τέλος) of their Christian life. It is this that our Lord meant when He said, "Be ye therefore (or, ye shall be) perfect, even as your Father which is in heaven is perfect" (Matt. v. 48). God is spoken of in the context of that verse as sending down His rain on the just and unjust, being kind indiscriminately to the unthankful and evil, and the Lord applies this to His disciples and says, "Do likewise, do not limit your attention to the good and beneficent. Be mature (and not immature) as is your Heavenly Father."

The precise form which Epaphras desired this maturity to take at Colosse was that they should stand "fully assured in all the will of God" (R.V.).

The will of God is the crown of life, and when a believer is "fully assured" concerning it, its clearness, its blessedness, its authority, then indeed is he making spiritual progress.

Toward this end prayer is the appointed means. Prayer develops spiritual faculties and leads to spiritual ripeness. Prayer makes real the presence of God, and in that presence the will of God becomes clear and asserts its complete yet blessed authority. The more we pray the riper we become and the more completely assured of the will of God in Christ Jesus concerning us. As a well-known writer, Dr. Schauffler, says, "When we are on our knees, then light flashes; then the intellect is clarified; then the conscience is aroused; then the spiritual sensibilities are quickened; and we can learn more of our duty and of His will than in hours of argumentation. So Jesus learned by prayer, and all He derived from men and nature was clarified and illuminated when the divine light came down as He was holding communion with His heavenly Father."

> "O Jesus Christ, grow Thou in me,
>   And all things else recede;
> My heart be daily nearer Thee,
>   From sin be daily freed.

Each day let Thy supporting might
My weakness still embrace;
My darkness vanish in Thy light,
Thy life my death efface.

In Thy bright beams which on me fall
Fade every evil thought;
That I am nothing, Thou art all,
I would be daily taught.

Make this poor self grow less and less,
Be Thou my life and aim;
O make me daily, through Thy grace,
More worthy of Thy Name."

Spiritual Power. Mark ix. 28, 29. "Lord, why could not we cast him out? . . . This kind cometh not out but by prayer . . ." There had been failure, dire and deplorable, on the part of the disciples in their Master's absence. A case of great need had been brought before them and they had utterly failed to expel the demon, notwithstanding the power previously given to them for this very purpose. The power was evidently not absolute but conditional, and they had forgotten to fulfill the condition and so maintain the power. The explanation of their failure is plainly told them by their Master. "This kind cometh not out but by prayer." They had failed in power because they had failed in prayer. If we would have power in service we must pray. The "demons" still to be found in our cities and villages, in our congregations and homes, will never be cast out except by prayer. "Lord, why is it my sermons are so powerless?" "Lord, how is it my Bible class lessons make no impression?" "Lord, why could I not lead those boys to Thee?" "This kind cometh not out but by prayer." We must prepare, but we must also pray. Our life of service must be permeated with prayer. Sermons, classes, visiting, open-air speaking, every form of Christian service must be suffused with prayer. Then will come power and blessing, with glory and praise to God.

Hitherto our aspirations in prayer have been concerned with ourselves and our own needs. We must now turn to the needs of others. A very large part of true Christianity is occupied with prayer for others.

Christian Fellowship. James v. 16. "Pray one for another." This is a call to pray for our friends and fellow-believers in Christ. God has so constituted the Church that a great part of our spiritual blessings are mediated through others, and especially through the prayers of others. Samuel had a very high idea of the importance of praying for others when he said, "God forbid that I should *sin against the Lord in ceasing to pray for you*" (1 Sam. xii. 23). The absence of intercessory prayer, then, is a *sin*. How solemn and searching this is! How many of us commit it by limiting our prayers too much to ourselves, our own life and its needs. And yet who that has tried it does not know the unspeakable joy that comes from bearing up before God the name of friend after friend in earnest, constant and believing prayer.

Some seem to find it a burden to do this. They have so many friends and acquaintances within their circle that it is quite impossible to bring them one by one to God and seek for definite blessing. They therefore content themselves with the most general and inclusive prayer for blessing and grace on their friends. But this is to lose blessing for themselves and for others. Intercessory prayer need not be a burden but a joy if we only set about it carefully and simply. A little book such as Dr. Harford's *Daily* or Dr. Andrew Murray's *Helps to Intercession* will enable us to spread the names of our friends over a week, or two weeks, or even a month, and so bring them before God without any difficulty and with ever-increasing delight. Best of all, if we prepare our own little book of intercessory prayer, according to our particular needs and circumstances, and then use it day by day in intercessory prayer, we shall find this exercise of our Christian priesthood (Heb. v. 1) one of the greatest joys and most special privileges of our Christian life. In addition to the blessings that will surely come to those for whom we pray we must never fail to remember the reflex benefits on our lives which come from seeking grace for others. "He that watereth shall be watered also himself" (Prov. xi. 25). Enlargement of soul, increase of sympathy, a deepening tenderness, a growing unselfishness, and a gradual conformity to the image of Him Whose main thought is (and was) always for others (Phil. ii. 8) will mark the life of the believer who makes prominent the work of intercessory prayer. "The Lord turned the captivity of Job *when* he prayed for his friends" (Job xlii. 10).

"The weary ones had rest, the sad had joy
    That day, and wondered 'how.'
A ploughman singing at his work had prayed,
    'Lord, help them now.'

Away in foreign lands they wondered how
    Their simple word had power.
At home, the Christians two or three had met
    To pray an hour.

Yes, we are always wond'ring, wond'ring 'how':
    Because we do not see
Someone, unknown perhaps, and far away,
    On bended knee!"

                            F. M. Nesbit.

The Ministry. 2 Thess. iii. 1. "Pray for us, that the Word of the Lord may run and be glorified." The Apostle Paul depended much and often on the prayers of his fellow-Christians. "Ye also helping together by prayer for us" (2 Cor. i. 11). Prayer for the ministry is one of the most pressing duties and one of the most blessed privileges of Christian people. Mr. Spurgeon was once asked how it was that he obtained such great blessings in his church. "My people pray for me," he replied. It is one of the joys and chief sources of power and encouragement in a minister's life to know that he is surrounded by a praying people. He knows and feels as he stands in the pulpit before the sermon commences that loving hearts are to be found in the congregation praying for the message he is about to deliver, and this gives him inspiration and power. And then to realise that during the week the concerns of the church and congregation are being daily brought before God by his congregation in private and family prayer is a guarantee of true fellowship and constant blessing on church life. A man cannot but preach with power if his people pray for him, and that church cannot help being a center of life and influence where the people are individually and unitedly waiting on God for spiritual blessing in the ministry. Some time ago a clergyman received

a letter from a stranger who said that sixty years
before she had received blessing in the particular
church to which the clergyman ministered. Since
then she had not failed to pray for the minister
and congregation every Sunday morning, and she
now wrote to enquire after the welfare of that
church and to know something of its affairs after
sixty years of absence and change. Who can tell
how much of the blessing which has been granted
to that church has been due to that old saint's
prayers? We cannot gauge the influence of our
prayers as we plead for the ministry that it may be
a ministry of power, that the Word preached may
"run and be glorified," and that the Gospel may
come not in word only, but also in power, and in
the Holy Ghost, and in much assurance (1 Thess.
i. 5).

World-wide Evangelisation. Matt. ix. 38.
"Pray ye therefore the Lord of the harvest, that He
will send forth labourers into His harvest." Why
"therefore"? Because "the harvest truly is plente-
ous, but the labourers are few" (v. 37). The place
of prayer in connection with missions is thus clear
and undoubted. One might think that in a work
calling for thought, energy, devotion, effort, the
need of prayer would be scarcely, if at all, felt.
But the Lord here makes it prominent, and bases it
on the greatness of the need and the fewness of the

supply of workers. And Christian experience universally bears witness to the power of prayer in connection with the evangelisation of the world. We sometimes hear it said in missionary sermons and addresses when appealing for more help, "If you can do nothing else for us, you can pray," as though prayer were the easiest thing in the world. It is in reality the hardest thing to do for foreign missions. It is much easier to read of missions, or to give, or even to go. If a man begins to pray for missions he will soon find that the expenditure of spiritual power and energy is by no means small, if his prayers are in any sense real. His prayers will lead to enquiry about missions, his inquiries will lead to knowledge, his knowledge to interest, his interest to sympathy, his sympathy to gifts, and his gifts to the consecration of his life to this paramount duty of the Christian Church. To pray definitely we must know something of the great field, for only thus can our prayers become definite, earnest, and certain of an answer.

Prayer for missions should be our daily work and joy. In connection with almost all our Missionary Societies there are Cycles of Prayer covering a week or a month, during which we can plead with God definitely and intelligently for the various parts of the great harvest field as well as

for the congregations at home where there are so
many Christians who at present are doing nothing
for their Master.   A strong, vigorous, growing
Christian life will always make daily prayer for
the evangelisation of the world a foremost duty,
and find in it a precious privilege and an increasing blessing.

The Church of Christ. Eph. vi. 17ff. "Praying
. . . for all saints." What a glorious conception
the Apostle gives us in Ephesians of the fellowship
of all Christians in the mystical Body of Christ
our Lord! That Epistle is essentially the Epistle
of the Church rather than of the individual, and in
addition to the teaching of the Epistle as a whole
(especially chapters i.-iv.) the phrase "all saints"
occurs twice to remind us of the place and power
of the whole community of Christians.   In chapter
iii. 18, 19, St. Paul prays that Christians may be
able to comprehend "with all saints what is the
breadth, and length, and depth, and height; and
to know the love of Christ."   All the saints are
required for this, for the love of Christ is beyond
the comprehension of any individual Christian.
From another point of view we see the importance
of the whole church when we are asked by the
Apostle to pray "for all saints."   Fellowship is
one of the most characteristic elements of true

Christianity, and the true life can only be lived aright in proportion as we seek to realise and benefit by the fullest possible fellowship among Christians. A solitary and purely individualistic Christianity is at once an impossibility, and an absolute contradiction of the very essence of the Gospel. The influence and blessing of the Church on the individual, and the corresponding action of the individual as part of the church are two sides of a great truth. We can readily understand, therefore, the necessity, power, and blessing of prayer for the whole church. Such prayer keeps the one who prays from narrowness, selfishness, and mere individualism, while the answer to the prayer blesses the church and enables it to realise more fully the purpose of God concerning it as a witness for Christ. Prayer "for all saints" should ever be prominent and persistent in our Christian life of prayer.

All the world. 1 Tim. ii. 1. "For all men." What a revelation of the heart of St. Paul we have in this verse; nay, more, what a revelation of the heart of God Who inspired the Apostle to write! What a revelation, too, of the power of prayer as embracing the whole world! God has indeed set the church a work to do in making supplication for all mankind. In this world-wide work of prayer

we find the true, deep meaning of the Christian
priesthood. A priest is defined as one who "is
ordained for men in things pertaining to God"
(Heb. v. 1). His work was pre-eminently associated with the offering of sacrifices and interces-
sions. The Christian Church as a whole, with each
Christian in particular, is now called upon to en-
gage in this holy work of priestly intercession.
From one point of view the Church is God's witness
to the world, bearing testimony to Him Whom the
world has rejected. In another sense, and with
equal reality, the Church brings the world before
God, bearing before the Throne of Grace its deep
needs, even though the great mass of mankind is
utterly unconscious of them. We are told of God's
attitude to the world in the very significant word
"philanthropy" (Titus iii. 4, Greek), *i.e.*, the love
of man as man, or "man-lovingness," as the late
Archbishop Benson once rendered it. It was the
same spirit of love for man as man that prompted
the barbarians at Melita to show the Apostle and
his companions no little "philanthropy" (Acts
xxviii. 2, Greek). How much more shall the Christian be a true "philanthropist," showing his love to
man in the best possible way by earnest, loving,
constant prayer for all men. And if we read the
context of the Apostolic injunction we shall have
a further truth of the power and scope of prayer.

"For kings, and for all that are in authority" (1 Tim. ii. 2). As Dr. Andrew Murray well says, "What a faith in the power of prayer! A few feeble and despised Christians are to influence the mighty Roman Emperors, and help in securing peace and quietness. Let us believe that prayer is a power that is taken up by God in His rule of the world. . . . When God's people unite in this they may count upon their prayer affecting in the unseen world more than they know."

"Lord, for the lonely heart
I pray apart.
Now, for this son of sorrow
Whom this to-morrow
Rejoiceth not, O Lord,
Hear my weak word.

For lives too bitter to be borne,
For the tempted and the torn,
For the prisoner in the cell,
For the shame lip doth not tell,
For the haggard suicide,
Peace, peace, this Christmastide.

In the desert, trod
By the long sick, O God;
Into the patient gloom
Of that small room
Where lies the child of pain
Of all neglected most—be fain
To enter, healing, and remain.

Now at the fall of day,
I bow and pray,
For those who cannot sleep
A watch I keep.

Oh, let the starving brain
Be fed and fed again;
At Thy behest
The tortured nerve find rest.

I see the vacant chair,
Father of souls, prepare
My poor thought's feeble power
To plead this hour:

For the empty, aching home,
Where the silent footsteps come,
Where the unseen face looks on,
Where the hand-clasp is not felt,
Where the dearest eyes are gone,
Where the portrait on the wall
Stirs and struggles as to speak,
Where the light breath from the hall
Calls the colour to the cheek,
Where the voice breaks in the hymn
When the sunset burneth dim,
Where the late large tear will start,
Frozen by the broken heart,
Where the lesson is to learn
How to live, to grieve, to yearn,
How to bear and how to bow.
Oh, the Christmas that is fled!
Lord of living and of dead,
    Comfort Thou!"

3. CONDITIONS OF PRAYER

Prayer must be *unceasing* (ἀδιαλείπτως), Rom. i.
9; 1 Thess. v. 17. What is the meaning of unceasing prayer? How is it possible to "pray
without ceasing"? The true idea is that of the
constant spirit of prayer which should character-
ise our life. The soul needs first of all its stated
times of prayer, day by day. These stated times
of prayer act as reservoirs of spiritual power
which influence the whole life. The result is that
the soul becomes permeated with spiritual force
and blessing which leads instinctively to a con-
tinual spirit of prayer and fellowship with God.

We use a picturesque and beautiful word when
we speak of "ejaculatory" prayer. It comes from
"jaculum," a dart or arrow, and fittingly describes
prayer which "darts" up to God at all times. This
is the true expression of the spirit of prayer, a
spirit which in any moment of opportunity lifts
itself up in a few words of prayer and intercession. Prayer, then, is at once an act and an
attitude, and as it has been well said, "Whatever
may be the attitude of the body the soul should be
ever on its knees." We may turn every circum-
stance, experience, and incident of the day into
prayer, and find in the "daily round, the common

task," constant opportunities of ascending to God in prayer and praise.

> "I need not leave the jostling world,
>   Or wait till daily tasks are o'er,
> To fold my palms in secret prayer
>   Within the close-shut closet door.
>
> There is a viewless, cloistered room,
>   As high as heaven, as fair as day,
> Where, though my feet may join the throng,
>   My soul can enter in and pray.
>
> And never through those crystal walls
>   The clash of life can pierce its way,
> Nor ever can a human ear
>   Drink in the spirit-words I say.
>
> One hearkening, even, cannot know
>   When I have crossed the threshold o'er;
> For He alone, Who hears my prayer,
>   Has heard the shutting of the door."

Prayer must be *steadfast* (προσκαρτερέω), "continuing instant," Rom. xii. 12. The word is used in several connections, all of which illustrate its meaning when applied to prayer. It is the word used of the little ship which was to "attend continually" on Jesus Christ" (Mark iii. 9), and it describes the attitude of Simon Magus in his "continuing" with Philip (Acts viii. 13). It is also used of those who were "waiting" for the day

of Pentecost (Acts i. 14), and the thought of the
word is that of someone putting forth his whole
strength in order to wait. It conveys at once the
idea of activity and passivity. It is well rendered
by the word "steadfast"—a state in which you put
forth your entire strength simply to wait. It
denotes the spirit of waiting continuously, stead-
fastly, upon God in prayer. We can see from all
this something of what prayer really means. It
calls for persistent activity and patient abiding,
the power of the whole soul being concentrated on
this blessed and fruitful experience.

Prayer must be *active* (ἀγωνίζομαι), Col. iv. 12;
(ἀγὼν) Col. ii. 1. The Greek words are rendered
exactly in English by our words "agonize" and
"agony." We sometimes speak of "agonizing in
prayer," but it is incorrect to associate the words
with the idea of pain, sharp pain, or suffering.
It is a word used not of pain, but of strenuous
effort in a contest; it is the activity of the wrestler
concentrating his whole energy on his effort; and
when St. Paul said of Epaphras that he was
always "agonizing in prayers" we must be careful
not to think of our English word, which implies
physical suffering. That is not in the Greek word
at all; the idea is of "a contest." You do not
imagine an athlete in positive pain when wrestling
or when endeavouring to win a race; he strains

every muscle to get to the winning-post, and puts
forth all his strength, vigour, and strenuousness.
We have great need of care when we speak of
our Lord being "in agony." No doubt our Lord
was in pain, but it is not included in that word
"agony." Ἀγωνία is a contest, a struggle with an
opponent, and therefore a putting forth of our
whole strength and vigour in that which we have
to do. When we thus take away the thought of
pain we remind believers that there is nothing
terrible, awful, and sad in praying, though there
is everything earnest, strenuous, determined, and
decided. It means that we should put forth all
our moral fibre and spiritual energy in order to
pray. And it also gives us more than a hint of
a strife, an effort on the part of our spiritual
adversary to prevent us from praying, and, still
more, from getting our prayers answered.

Prayer must be *intense* (ἐκτενῶς, ἐκτενέστερον),
Acts xii. 5; Luke xxii. 44. The above are the only
two passages where the word is used in relation
to prayer. It comes from ἐκτείνω, "to stretch out,"
and implies an intensity by which we nerve ourselves, and, as it were, stretch ourselves out in
order to do our very utmost in prayer. It implies
a bow drawn to its full length and strength. So
should our hearts be in prayer.

Once more, then, we see what prayer really

means as an element of true spiritual life and
experience. It is no mere spiritual luxury to be
enjoyed or not at will. It is the outgoing of every
faculty of our spiritual being in a whole-hearted
approach to God.

At this point it is possible that someone thinking of these four words—"incessant," "steadfast,"
"active," "intense"—is saying, "This is too great
a demand in the strain which it puts upon me.
This is emphasizing the human side of prayer to
such an extent that it is beyond me. Not only are
my past prayers rebuked, but my future prayers
seem hopeless." But in reply it should be remem-
bered that God knows our need, and shows us the
human side in order to reveal to us the divine side
also. As we continue the consideration of these
conditions of prayer we shall see how wonderfully
God Himself provides for the fulfilment of these
requirements.

Prayer must be *submissive*. 1 John v. 14.
"According to His will." Prayer is necessarily
based on God's revelation of Himself and His will.
His promises encourage and His commands incite
us to prayer. At the same time the will of God
gives us the due and necessary limit of prayer.
There are many things for which we never think
of asking, simply because they are not only not
included in, but are clearly opposed to, His re-

vealed will. There are other matters about which we are certain that they are according to His will, and as to these we plead His promises and continue praying, waiting, expecting the answer in God's good time. Yet again, there are many things about which there is no revelation in the Word of God, and with reference to these we pray in submission to the will of God, and wait His way of revealing to us in daily circumstances and experience whether the prayer is in harmony with His purpose concerning us. This spirit of submissiveness is one of the primary conditions of prayer and one of the essential marks of a true spiritual life. Our Lord, in Gethsemane, prayed in this spirit, "Not My will, but Thine be done," and when the soul is ready to trust God fully and rest on His perfect wisdom, the joyous experience is that of the Apostle when he said, "This is the confidence that we have in Him, that, if we ask anything according to His will, He heareth us" (1 John v. 14).

> "If when I kneel to pray,
> With eager lips I say:
> 'Lord, give me all the things that I desire;
> Health, wealth, fame, friends, brave hearts, religious fire,
> The power to sway my fellow-men at will,
> And strength for mighty works to banish ill';
> In such a prayer as this,
> The blessing I must miss.

Or if I only dare
To raise this fainting prayer:
'Thou seest, Lord, that I am poor and weak,
And cannot tell what things I ought to seek;
I therefore do not ask at all, but still
I trust Thy bounty all my wants to fill';
My lips shall thus grow dumb,
The blessing will not come.

But if I lowly fall,
And thus in faith I call:
'Through Christ, O Lord, I pray Thee give to me,
Not what I would, but what seems best to Thee,
Of life, of health, of service, and of strength,
Until to Thy full joy I come at length';
My prayer shall then avail,
The blessing will not fail."

Prayer must be *in the name of Christ.* John
xiv. 13; xvi. 24: "In My Name." The "Name"
of Christ is the revelation of His Person and
Character. It is not a mere title, but the expression of everything we know of Him. The "Name"
is the nature, so far as we possess the manifesta-
tion of it. "In His Name" implies union and
communion with Him. And "praying in His
Name" means asking in union and fellowship with
Him as the sphere and atmosphere of our life.
Our Lord had taught His disciples many lessons
on prayer from the beginning of His ministry, but

this lesson of praying "in His Name" was a new one (John xvi. 24) and marked an advance on their former knowledge and experience. In these chapters of St. John (xiv.—xvii.) we have several references to the "Name" of Christ, and to the blessings associated with it. The more fully we get to know the Lord in the plentitude and power of His presence and grace, the more truly we shall be enabled to pray "in His Name." The Word of God carefully and constantly studied will reveal to us more of the "fulness of the blessing of Christ," and this will make our prayers richer, fuller, deeper, and more closely in union with the will and purpose of God. We shall enter more deeply into fellowship with our Lord as He pleads above, and our prayers will bring power and blessing to all for whom we pray. Let us take time to learn from God the increasing and infinite possibilities of prayer "in the Name" of our Lord Jesus Christ.

Prayer must be *in the Spirit*. Jude 20, "Praying in the Holy Ghost"; Eph. vi. 18, "Praying . . . in the Spirit." This condition shows at once the Divine requirement and provision in relation to prayer. The indwelling of the Holy Spirit is the unspeakable blessing of every believer's life, and this Divine presence is intimately connected with our life of prayer. The Holy Spirit pleads within us (Rom. viii. 26), and we in turn "pray in the Holy Spirit." The word "Advocate" as applied to our Lord (1 John ii. 1) and the word "Comforter" as applied to the Spirit are the same, and the meaning is "one called to help." The Advocate above pleads before the Throne, the Advocate within pleads in our hearts, and thus we are linked to the Throne of God and are enabled to pray in the Holy Spirit. He reveals our needs, prompts our petitions, influences our desires, strengthens our faith, and confirms our hope and expectation of answers to our prayers. The more fully we can realise our union and communion with the Holy Spirit the more we shall experience the joy and power of "praying with all prayer and supplication in the Spirit." It is because we are living and praying in the Holy Spirit that we are enabled to fulfill all the other conditions and pray incessantly, actively, strenuously, and intensely.

Thus the human side of prayer is met by the Divine, and if we are abiding in the Holy Ghost we shall be enabled to put forth all these activities, and prayer will not only not be a burden, but on the contrary a positive delight and a genuine blessing.

"Lord, I have shut my door!
Come Thou and visit me; I am alone!
Come, as when doors were shut, Thou cam'st of yore,
       And visitedst Thine own.
My Lord, I kneel with reverent love and fear,
       For Thou art here."

4. ACCOMPANIMENTS OF PRAYER

There are several things recorded in the New Testament as associated with prayer, and a careful study of them will be of great service in learning how to pray.

Prayer must be accompanied by *faith* (πίστις), Mark xi. 24. This is the inevitable and essential accompaniment of all true prayer. Prayer must be based on Divine Revelation and find its warrant in the promises and assurances of God's love and grace. This distinguishes Christian prayer from everything that goes by the name of prayer in heathen religions. Christian prayer is based on the Word of God. God encourages, commands, invites, welcomes prayer. The charter of prayer was given by our Lord at the outset of His ministry. "Ask, and it shall be given you; seek, and ye shall find; knock, and it shall be opened unto you." This charter was confirmed again and again through His earthly ministry until it found its crown in His fullest, deepest teaching on Prayer on the eve of the Crucifixion, when, as we

have seen, He taught His disciples the meaning
of prayer: "in My Name." This warrant of
prayer is accordingly met by our response of trust.
Our faith accepts the assurance that prayer will
be heard and answered, and pleads the fulfillment
of Divine promises. Faith is thus the only possible response to the Divine revelation, and apart
from our belief in God as the Hearer of prayer
there could not be any real prayer or genuine
blessing. "He that cometh to God must believe
that He is, and that He is a rewarder of them that
diligently seek Him" (Heb. xi. 6). Herein lies
the intimate and necessary connection between the
Word of God and Prayer. The greater our knowledge of the Scriptures and the richer our experience of its preciousness, the fuller and deeper will
be our prayers, until it shall become the simplest
and most natural and most instructive experience
of our life to live in the Divine Presence and rest
on the Divine promises, and then to pour out our
souls in the prayer of faith and believe to see the
goodness of the Lord in the land of the living.

Prayer must be accompanied by *frankness*
(παρρησία). In 1 John v. 14, the word is rendered
"confidence," and means "freedom of speech," or
"unreserved conversation" as between those who
fully trust each other. This word occurs four
times in St. John's first Epistle, twice with refer-

ence to the believer in relation to the future, and twice in relation to the present. It is helpful to render it in 1 John ii. 28, as giving the true meaning, by "And now, little children, abide in Him; that, when He shall appear, we may *tell Him everything,* and not be ashamed before Him at His coming." Our true attitude at that day will be "freedom of speech," nothing between us, nothing kept back. We find the same word in chapter iv. 17, "That we may have *boldness* in the day of judgment" ($\pi\alpha\rho\rho\eta\sigma\iota\alpha$). Also in chapter iii. 21, "Beloved, if our hearts condemn us not, then have we *confidence* (boldness) towards God." And then chapter v. 14, "This is the *confidence* we have in Him, that if we ask anything according to His will, He heareth us." When we kneel in prayer this should be the spirit of our approach to God, a spirit of confidence, of unreserved speech, which tells Him everything, and a spirit of child-like faith and assurance which rests on His promises and expects their fulfillment in answer to prayer.

Prayer must be accompanied by *fasting* (Acts xiv. 23). From time to time in the New Testament prayer and fasting are associated (cf. Mark ix. 29). In these passages the references are doubtless to abstinence from food, but we may well believe that fasting from food is only one precise way in which the spiritual action associated with the idea is to be expressed. Fasting represents an attitude of *detachment* from the things of time and sense whether it be from food, or pleasure, or lawful ambition. Prayer represents the complementary attitude of *attachment* to the things of God and the spiritual world. When we thus realise our need of detachment from earth we shall readily determine, under the guidance of the Holy Spirit, what particular forms our fasting shall take. In the times of our Puritan forefathers the spiritual value of fasting from food was fully realised, and there can be no doubt whatever of the relation of physical food to spiritual blessing. The sin of overeating is only too apt to hinder spiritual power in prayer, while if we "keep under the body" we shall certainly be conscious of more liberty and blessing as we fulfill our work of prayer and intercession. What we need concerning food, dress, books, recreation, friendship, ambition, is the resolute determination to be above them, superior to them, in order that the spiritual may rule everything. Like St. Paul, we should say, "All things are lawful for me, but I will not be brought under the power of any" (1 Cor. vi. 12). This is the true idea of fasting, and in this spirit of detachment from things earthly we obtain one of the true accompaniments of, and helps to, that spirit of attachment to God which is found in prayer.

Prayer must be accompanied by *watching*. "Watching thereunto with all perseverance" (Eph. vi. 18); "Continue in prayer, and watch in the same with thanksgiving" (Col. iv. 2). There are two words rendered by our word "watch"; one simply means "the absence of sleep," and the other "expectation." This "watching" is associated with prayer in a number of passages. But what does it mean? It is very suggestive and significant to notice that in the New Testament we never find any object attached to the word "watch." We are never told what to watch. It does not say, "Watch your enemies," or "Watch Satan," or even "Watch yourselves." The word is absolutely free grammatically from any definite object; and this may be intended to teach us we are to be concerned only with watching *Christ*. Not looking in, watching our sins; not looking round, watching our enemies—we shall get baffled if we watch them; not looking round and watching men; but watching Christ, "looking unto Jesus." If we look into our hearts we shall despair; but if we look to Christ we shall see ourselves as He sees us, and we shall see the precious blood and the merit of the atoning sacrifice. Occupied with Him we shall be guarded, guided, and blessed in all things, and

be enabled to wait in expectation of His answers
to our prayer. So "watching unto prayer," our
eyes will be fixed on Christ in an attitude of expectation, looking off from everything else to Him,
and waiting His answers to our petitions. "I will
direct my prayer unto Thee, and will *look up*"
(Psalm v. 3). May this ever be the necessary
accompaniment to our prayer.

Prayer must be accompanied by *obedience* (1
John iii. 22). We obtain our petitions because we
obey God and do what is pleasing in His sight.
This does not mean that obedience is the ground of
answered prayer, for God's mercy and love are
the only foundation of blessing. It means that
only in an obedient spirit can we expect blessing.
It would be incongruous and impossible for us to
pray and expect answers while our lives are out
of harmony with God and we are living in dis-
obedience to His will. "If I regard iniquity in
my heart, the Lord will not hear me." When the
soul is true to God blessing inevitably comes, for
obedience is ever one of the pathways to power
in prayer.

Prayer must be accompanied by *forgiveness*
(Mark xi. 25). The necessity of forgiveness of
our fellow-Christians and of all men is frequently
emphasised by our Lord and also by His Apostles
(Matt. vi. 14; Mark xi. 25; Eph. iv. 32; Col. iii.

13). In the Lord's Prayer we are taught to ask for God's forgiveness, since we ourselves have the spirit of forgiveness which we desire to receive ourselves. If there is any grudge or resentment in the heart, to say nothing of anger and malice, there is no possibility of prayer being answered. If we should say, "I forgive but I cannot forget," it may well mean that we do not really forgive after all. Without a sincere and hearty spirit of loving forgiveness there cannot possibly be any power in prayer, and the Lord's word stands out clear and sharp. "When ye stand praying, forgive."

Prayer must be accompanied by *thanksgiving*. Philippians iv. 6 is one among many passages. "In everything by prayer and supplication with thanksgiving, let your request be made known unto God." Why is thanksgiving so frequently associated with prayer? There must be some reason for it. If we look at St. Paul's Epistles we very seldom find the one mentioned without the other. It is probably intended to suggest the attitude of appropriation as well as of supplication. Prayer is asking; thanksgiving is testifying that we have received. It is just here that we fail; we ask, but we do not accept and appropriate. Faith in Scripture is two-fold in meaning. There is the faith that *asks* and the faith that *accepts*. The

faith that asks is expressed in prayer, the faith
that accepts is expressed in thanksgiving. We
are continually asking, but have we the faith
that appropriates? A Christian man went to
lunch with an intimate friend whom he had known
for twenty-five years, and after "grace" was said,
the ordinary phrase being used, asking to be "made
truly thankful," the guest, claiming the privilege
of friendship, enquired, "When do you expect to
get that prayer answered? You have been praying all these years to be *made* thankful!" The
man had been "asking," but never appropriating.
He had the faith that asks, but not the faith that
accepts. Many a Christian would find life more
powerful and blessed if he knew a little more of
the faith that appropriates, faith that expresses
itself in thanksgiving, "O God, I *thank* Thee!"
We may see this in the Revised Version of Mark
xi. 24, "Whatsoever things ye desire when ye pray,
believe that ye *have received* them, and ye shall
have them." Let us not fail to accompany our
prayer with this appropriation of thanksgiving.

Prayer must be accompanied by *joy*. "Making
request with joy" (Phil. i. 4). In some respects
this is the deepest and most inclusive element.
When we come before God our prayer should be
accompanied with inward satisfaction, because we
are going to meet our God and are sure of His

blessing. We should experience the very opposite
of pain or anguish, and have the consciousness of
a privilege, a joy, in approaching God.   There is
no joy like the joy of living in the presence of
God, the joy of asking Him for what we need, the
joy of receiving His blessed answers to our prayers. It is the joy of joys to realise our true position before Him, and to be assured of power in
prayer. It is the joy of a great peace, the joy
of a holy privilege, the joy of a perpetual fellowship, the joy of a perfect satisfaction.

> "My inmost soul, O Lord, to Thee
>   Leans like a growing flower
> Unto the light; I do not know
>   The day nor blessed hour
> When that deep-rooted, daring growth
>   We call the heart's desire
> Shalt burst and blossom to a prayer
>   Within the sacred fire
> Of Thy great patience; grow so pure,
>   So still, so sweet a thing
> As perfect prayer must surely be.
>   And yet my heart will sing
> Because Thou seem'st sometimes so near.
>   Close-present God! to me,
> It seems I could not have a wish
>   That was not shared by Thee;
> It seems I cannot be afraid
>   To speak my longings out,
> So tenderly Thy gathering love
>   Enfolds me round about;

It seems as if my heart would break,
    If, living on the light,
It should not lift to Thee at last
    A bud of flawless white.
And yet, O helpless heart! how sweet
    To grow, and bud, and say:
'The flower, however marred or wan,
    Shall not be cast away.' "

We have now considered the main lines of Scripture teaching on the subject of prayer, though only the fringe of a vast territory has been touched. By means of a concordance we may work out more fully for ourselves these lines of meditation and study, and find in them the source of increasing spiritual blessing.

If anyone should inquire how such a life of prayer is possible, the answer is clear and unmistakable. For this attitude of prayer we must have times of prayer. The attitude is based on acts, and times of prayer are necessary as the occasions of storage and accumulation of light, and power, and grace. Let us see to it that not a day passes without definitely going aside with God for solitary prayer.

How shall we commence? Let us start with five minutes only. Opening our Bible with a prayer for God's illumination, let us read a verse or short passage as the message of God to our souls. Then we may turn the verse into prayer and thus spend those five minutes with God. Let us do this again the next day, and again the day after. We should not go beyond the five minutes until these are fully enjoyed. It will not be long before we shall be conscious of spiritual illumination and satisfaction as we wait before God in prayer, and very soon our five minutes will be extended. We shall enjoy this time so much that the minutes will be all too short, and we shall find it possible to do that easiest of all things in the world, *make time!*

It is this failure to spend a definite, even though it be short, time each day with God that is the secret of all weakness, variableness, and shallowness in our spiritual experience and service. We sometimes sing,

> "Oh, the pure delight of a single hour
> That before Thy Throne I spend."

A *single hour!* How often do we do it? How many of us do it? A *single hour!* And yet we hurry over our prayer-time and fail to give God one-quarter of a single hour. Of course He only expects the "hour" if we really can give it, and it is wonderful how much prayer we can put into five minutes and how much blessing we can get out of it if only these few minutes are practicable

for us. Our time may not be long, but it must
be regular; and from the act will come the habit,
and from the habit the attitude, and from the
attitude the character, settled, strong, sure, and
abiding, wherein God's presence will be more and
more a delight, and God's power more and more
realized.

> "When thou wakest in the morning,
>   Ere thou tread the untried way
> Of the lot that lies before thee
>   Through the coming busy day,
> Whether sunbeams promise brightness,
>   Whether dim forebodings fall,
> Be thy dawning glad or gloomy,
>   Go to Jesus—tell Him all.
>
> In the calm of sweet communion
>   Let thy daily work be done,
> In the peace of soul outpouring
>   Care be banished, patience won.
> And if earth with its enchantments
>   Seek thy spirit to enthrall,
> Ere thou listen—ere thou answer,
>   Turn to Jesus—tell Him all.
>
> Then as hour by hour glides by thee
>   Thou wilt blessed guidance know.
> Thine own burden being lightened,
>   Thou canst bear another's woe.
> Thou canst help the weak ones onward,
>   Thou canst raise up those that fall,
> But remember, while thou servest,
>   Still tell Jesus—tell Him all.

And if weariness creeps o'er thee
  As the day wears to its close,
Or if sudden fierce temptations
  Bring thee face to face with foes,
In thy weakness, in thy peril,
  Raise to heaven a trustful call,
Strength and calm for every crisis
  Come—in telling Jesus all."

                        G. M. Taylor.